Christ Jesus, the Way

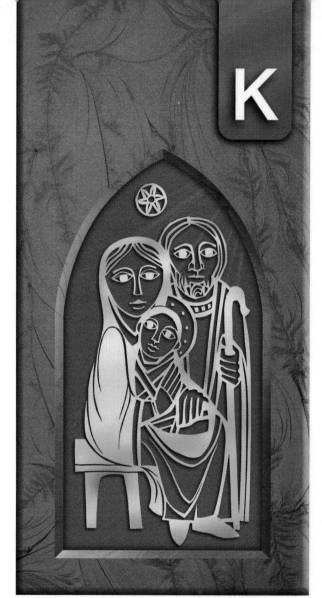

K

General Editors

Sister Catherine Dooley, O.P.
Rev. Berard Marthaler, OFM Conv.
Rev. Gerard P. Weber

Consulting Editors

Monsignor Thomas McDade, Ph.D.
Irene Murphy
David Michael Thomas, Ph.D.

D1401364

Benziger

Woodland Hills, California

Credits

Total Parish Catechesis: William Huebsch

Educational Consultants: Anne Battes Kirby, Barbara Kay Bowie, Judy Deckers

Consultants: Clare Collela; Dr. Peter Gilmour, Ph.D.; Rev. Robert Hater, Ph.D.; Sr. Ann Laszok, CSBM (Eastern Catholics); Sister Eva Marie Lumas, SSS; Rev. Ronald Nuzzi, Ph.D.; Daniel Pierson; Rev. Peter Phan, Ph.D.; Art Zannoni (Sacred Scripture)

Contributors: Christina DeCamp, Silvia DeVillers, Sandy Lauzon, Camille Liscinsky, Joanne McPortland; Yvette Nelson, Catherine M. Odell, Dee Ready, Charles Savitskas, Margaret Savitskas, Susan Stark, Helen Whitaker

Mission Education: Maryknoll Fathers, Brothers, and Sisters

Liturgical Catechesis: Sr. Catherine Dooley, OP (General Editor); Maria Elena Cardena; Silvia DeVillers; Sr. Miriam Malone, SNJM; Ret Siefferman; Joan Vos

Liturgy: Rev. John Gallen, SJ

Music Editors: Gary Daigle, Jaime Cortez

Video: Dr. Thomas Boomershine, Ph.D.; Amelia Cooper

Design: Bill Smith Studios, Monotype Composition

Production: Monotype Composition

Cover Design: Robert Hyre and Logan Design

Cover Art: Br. Stephen Erspamer, SM

International Photography: Maryknoll Magazine

Nihil Obstat: Sr. Karen Wilhelmy, CSJ, Censor Deputatus

Imprimatur: † Roger Cardinal Mahony, Archbishop of Los Angeles, September 19, 2001

The nihil obstat and imprimatur are official declarations that the work contains nothing contrary to Faith and Morals. It is not implied thereby that those who have granted the nihil obstat and imprimatur agree with the contents, statements, or opinions expressed.

Send all inquiries to:
Benziger
21600 Oxnard St., Suite 500
Woodland Hills, CA 91367

ISBN 0-07-821712-1
Printed in the United States of America
1 2 3 4 5 6 7 8 9 073 06 05 04 03 02 01

Christ Jesus, the Way

The Ad Hoc Committee
to Oversee the Use of the Catechism,
United States Conference of Catholic Bishops,
has found the student editions of
Christ Jesus, the Way
to be in conformity
with the *Catechism of the Catholic Church.*

Contents

Know, Love, Serve · A Little Catechism　　　　**7**

　Welcome!　　　　8

　Follow Jesus　　　　9

　Know　　　　10

　Love　　　　12

　Serve　　　　14

Unit One · God Loves Me　　　　**16**

　1　I Am Special　　　　17

　2　All about Me　　　　23

　3　Feelings　　　　29

　4　God's Love　　　　35

　Unit Review　　　　41

Unit Two · I Love God　　　　**42**

　5　Jesus　　　　43

　6　Good Words　　　　49

　7　Good Things to Do　　　　55

　8　I Can Pray　　　　61

　Unit Review　　　　67

Unit Three · I Love Others　　　　**68**

　9　My Family　　　　69

　10　Friends　　　　75

　11　Being Together　　　　81

　12　Caring for Animals　　　　87

　Unit Review　　　　93

Unit Four • Church   **94**

13   I Belong   95

14   My Parish   101

15   My Father's House   107

16   I Am Catholic   113

Unit Review   119

Unit Five • Celebrate   **120**

17   Memory   121

18   Being Alive   127

19   Holy Days   133

20   The Mass   139

Unit Review   145

Unit Six • Caring   **146**

21   Be a Helper!   147

22   Care   153

23   Caring for You   159

24   The Good of All   165

Unit Review   171

Celebrate!   **172**

Mother Mary   173

All Saints   175

Advent   177

Christmas   179

Lent   181

Easter   183

Summer   185

Contents

Your ABCs   **187**

Certificate   **189**

I Do Believe!   **190**

Acknowledgments   **191**

Craft Pages   **193**

Craft 1: Who Am I?   193

Craft 2: I Can See   195

Craft 3: God Made Animals   197

Craft 4: The Lion and the Mouse   199

Craft 5: Praying Hands   201

Craft 6: My House   203

Craft 7: Friends   205

Craft 8: Caring for Animals   207

Craft 9: Build a Church   209

Craft 10: The Sign of the Cross   211

Craft 11: Baptism   213

Craft 12: Go Forth!   215

Craft 13: A Helping Hand   217

Craft 14: A Good Night's Sleep   219

Craft 15: Grow a Flower   221

Craft 16: The Clever Caterpillar   223

Know Love Serve

A Little Catechism

Let the children come to me. The kingdom of God belongs to such as these.

Mark 10:14

Welcome!

This year you will learn about God!
What a happy year it will be.

Follow Jesus

Please read to me.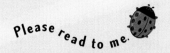

Mary and Joseph traveled to Bethlehem. They went there to be counted. While they were there, Jesus was born. Mary and Joseph laid him in a manger because there was no room for them in the inn. Shepherds came to visit the baby. The angels sang, "Glory to God in heaven and peace to his people on earth."

Based on *Luke 2:1–14*

I love you, Jesus.
You are my friend!

The Blessed Mother

Mary was the mother of Jesus.
Mary helped Jesus learn and grow.
Mary will help you, too.
You can call Mary "Mother."

Saint Joseph

Joseph was Jesus' father.
Joseph kept Jesus safe.
Jesus helped Joseph.
You can ask Joseph to help you
follow Jesus.

Talking with God

Sh! Be quiet!
God is talking to you.
Hear the stories.
Hear the love.
You can hear messages from above.
Sh! Be quiet!
God is talking to you.

Speak up!
God is listening to you.
Say you are happy.
Say you are sad.
Say you are sorry if you've been bad.
Speak up!
God is listening to you.

From your friends
at Maryknoll

Two Prayers

Here are two prayers you can learn by heart.

The Sign of the Cross

In the name of the Father,
and of the Son,
and of the Holy Spirit.
Amen.

A Night Prayer

God be with me as I sleep.
Bless those who love and
    care for me.
I love you, dear God.
I know you love me, too.

Show You Care

I use my hands to show I care.
I use my feet to show I care.
I use my eyes and my ears, too.
I use my mouth to say "I will
   help you."
Put them all together.
See how much I care!

All around the World

The friends of Jesus travel.
They travel to the mountains.
They travel to the sea.
They travel where it's hot.
And they travel where it's cold.
They tell people how much God
    loves them all!

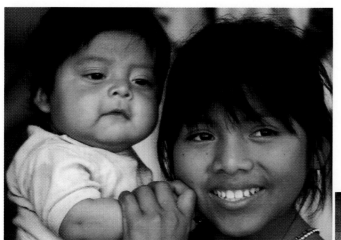

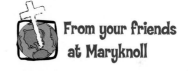

From your friends
at Maryknoll

God calls you each by name.

Psalm 147:4

Cambodia

 From Maryknoll

God Loves Me

Chapter

1 I Am Special

2 All about Me

3 Feelings

4 God's Love

I AM SPECIAL

God loves you!

John 16:27

WHO DO I SEE?

Oh, look and see!

Who can it be?

It's someone special.

It must be me!

GOD MADE ME

God made all people.
God made me.
Everyone is special.

A Happy Song!

Sing and clap this song.

I'm so happy that God made me,
   yes, I am.
I'm so happy that God made me,
   yes, I am.
I'm so happy that God made me.
I'm so happy that God made me.
I'm so happy that God made me,
   yes, I am.

Look at Me

Look at me.

Who do you see?

Is that me with hair as

 as  ?

No!

My hair is

as as .

as as a .

as as a .

as as a

Look at me.

Who do you see?

Is that me with eyes as

 as the ?

No!

My eyes are

as as  .

as as a .

as as the  .

GOD LOVES ME!

No matter what I look like or the
  color of my skin,
No matter what my name is or the
  mess my room is in,
God loves me this much
  (spread your arms as wide as you can)
  just the way I am!

GOD LOVES YOU!

Stand with a friend.
Spread your arms wide.
Say to the friend,
"God loves you this much."

WE PRAY

God, you give me wonderful gifts!

You guide me, and you are always

with me.

You love me very much.

You make me so happy!

Based on *Psalm 16:5–9*

GOD LOVES ME!

Dear Family,

How wonderful it is that you have a child in kindergarten, an age of cheerfulness and enthusiasm! Welcome to *Christ Jesus, the Way*. Your child's first formal religion class this year began with a positive message—I am special. Here are ways to bring the message into your home.

At Home

You are the most important person in your child's world. Your praise means more to him or her than anyone else's. If there are several children in your family, make sure that each one has opportunities to feel special. Making a child's special meal, making a "date" to do something together, even sitting a few moments to listen and respond to a silly story, all help to build your child's self-esteem.

Sharing Faith

When you show love to your child, you are expressing a simple, yet powerful, truth: "You are special, and God loves you." Help develop this understanding in your child. Share your faith in simple ways. When you say "I love you" to your child, add now and then, "And God loves you, too."

Habits of Faith

Tolerance. There's a poem in chapter 1 that teaches a basic Christian value: God loves us just the way we are. Guide your child to be accepting of others. Model nonjudgmental behavior.

Bible Verse. Each letter you receive will have a Bible verse from your child's lesson. Cut out the verse and display it in your home. Put the verse at your child's eye level. Help your child read and learn the words of the verse. Soon, learning the words of the Bible will come as easily to your child as learning the words to a favorite song.

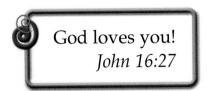

God loves you!
John 16:27

All about Me

Watch Me

I can do many things.
Hooray!
Look at me!
I can count—

_____, _____, _____.

Yippee!
Here I go—
Up in the air,
Then down real low.

A Wonderful Body

God gave me my body.
My body helps me know the world.
Look what I can do with my body.

I Can Taste!

Tasty noodles slip inside.
Slurp! Slurp! Slurp!

I Can Hear!

The door shuts with a slam.
Wham! Bam! Bam!

I Can See!

The sun bursts through the clouds.
Ooh! Ooh! Ooh!

I Can Smell!

With my nose I sniff and smell.
Sometimes I sneeze.
Achoo!

I Can Touch!

My toes wiggle in the mud.
Squish! Squish! Squish!

MY WONDERFUL MIND

God gave me a mind.
I use my mind to think.
Look what I can do.

1. I know what shape comes next.

2. I can write the missing letters.

A B C D E

3. I can write the missing numbers.

1 2 3 4 5

ABOUT ME

I am special.
I'll tell you why.
Here's one thing I can do.

Thank you, God,

for my   and ,

for my and

and and .

Thank you for my

wonderful mind

that helps me learn

and be so kind.

Amen.

Dear Family,

Chapter 2 is titled "All about Me." The chapter focuses on an awareness of the wonderful body and the marvelous mind that are God's gifts.

At Home

The brain is constantly developing and growing cells. Keep your child's brain stimulated with new experiences, particularly activities in which your child has a part. For example, even when you read a story, you can ask, "What do you think will happen next?" Or ask what-if questions: "What if Cinderella hadn't lost her glass slipper?"

Play is more than fun for children; play is actually the way children learn best. You can stay right in your own home and provide plenty of opportunities for the physical and mental exploration of new things.

Sharing Faith

When you are tucking in your child for the night, talk about the good things that happened during the day. End by saying a Bible verse or telling your child a short Bible story.

Habits of Faith

Respect for God's Gifts. Encourage your child to respect the body and the mind. Provide sedentary activities—reading, drawing, coloring, puzzle-making. Play hide-and-seek or follow the leader, catch a ball, or take a walk.

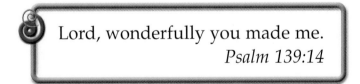

Lord, wonderfully you made me.
Psalm 139:14

FEELINGS

GLAD AND SAD

Draw Sally's mouth.
Show how she feels.

Silly Sally is oh so glad.

Silly Sally is oh so sad.

Feelings · 29

MANY FEELINGS

God gave me feelings.
God wants me to be happy.
I can talk to God about
my feelings.

Tell how you would feel.

Someone is sick.

You have a new pet.

Your new toy is broken.

The lights go out.

You see a rainbow.

HAPPY SAD SUPRISED ANGRY

Other People's Feelings

Other people have feelings, too.
Draw a line to show how the
  feeling happened.
Who needs to feel better?
What could you say?

SHOWING FEELINGS

Circle some ways that you show feelings.

ZACCHAEUS

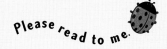 Please read to me.

1. Zacchaeus collected tax money from people. They thought he took too much.

2. People shouted, "Jesus is coming!" Zacchaeus was too short to see.

3. Zacchaeus climbed a tree to see. Jesus said, "Zacchaeus, I would like to have dinner with you!"

4. Zacchaeus said, "I am sorry for anything I did wrong. I will give money to the poor." Then Zacchaeus gave a big party.

Based on *Matthew 19:1–10*

Talk about each picture.

How did each person feel?

We Pray

Dear God, help me make others feel happy and good. Amen.

Dear Family,

Part of what makes people wonderful is their ability to show feelings. Chapter 3 focuses on God's gift of feelings. Your child was guided to use words that describe feelings, to discover appropriate ways to express feelings, and to realize that other people have feelings, too.

At Home

Expressing feelings is healthy for people of all ages. Adults find it easier to express feelings properly if they were shown how to do so as children. The first step in expressing feelings is naming them. Model ways your child can express feelings by naming them. "I feel sad today because Toby is sick."

Sharing Faith

Be sensitive to other people. When people need to feel better, to have their spirits lifted, come up with ideas you and your child can do. "Grandma is feeling lonely. Let's give her a call."

Habits of Faith

Handling Anger. It's okay to be angry. It's the way you express your anger that can become a problem! Give your child ways to show anger appropriately—socking a pillow or going to a quiet, private place. Make clear what actions are inappropriate and why they are unacceptable.

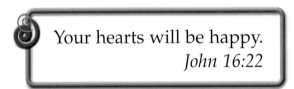

> Your hearts will be happy.
> *John 16:22*

God's Love

Look and See

Look out the window.

What do you see?

A bird?

The sky?

A tree?

God made all three!

God said, "Everything I have made is good."

Genesis 1:31

I See God's Love

God made the world.
I cannot see God.
But I can see God's love.

I FEEL GOD'S LOVE

God is always with me.

People love me and care for me.

They show me God's love.

Put a heart around all the people

showing God's love.

AN ACTION PRAYER

Thank you, God, for tall, tall trees

(Reach up high.)

And tiny little flowers.

(Put hands close to ground.)

Thank you, God, for sunshine

(Reach high and spread fingers wide.)

And for cool, rainy showers.

(Bring hands down, fluttering fingers.)

Thank you, God, for oceans deep

(Touch hands to floor.)

And for your mountains high.

(Stand on tiptoes.)

Thank you, God, for little birds.

(Flap arms.)

Thank you, God, for loving friends.

(Point to others.)

And thank you, God, for me!

(Point to self.)

Dear Family,

We know God's love for us through the people who love and care for us, and through the beauty of creation. Chapter 4 helped your child see that the earth and all the good things in it are signs of God's love.

At Home

Stop to enjoy the marvels of God's creation. Grow a plant. Watch the sunset. Look at the stars. Take a walk. Stop and feel the sturdiness of tree bark, smell the scent of a flower, share the shapes you see in the cloud formations. If your child is learning colors, the outdoors is a perfect place to practice their names. "Touch something that's green."

Sharing Faith

As your child grows to recognize God as the Creator, your child will learn that God is the source of all beauty and life. Look for a time to share a personal story that shows you appreciate the beauty of God's creation. You may tell about a special bouquet of flowers you once enjoyed or about a giant weeping willow that you played under as a child.

Habits of Faith

Care for the Environment. God gave people dominion over plants and animals. You are caretakers. Use everyday opportunities to model behavior that helps to preserve the environment. Recycle cans, plastic, and paper at home. Show your child how to dispose of litter properly when away from home.

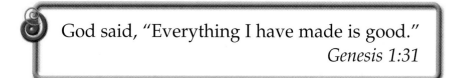

God said, "Everything I have made is good."
Genesis 1:31

GOD LOVES ME

I Am Special

All about Me

MAX THE MAGNIFICIENT

Feelings

God's Love

Jesus grew and became strong.

Luke 2:40

Cuba

 From Maryknoll

I Love God

Chapter

5 Jesus

6 Good Words

7 Good Things to Do

8 I Can Pray

Jesus

Jesus said, "Come, follow me."

Mark 10:21

Let's Go!

Make up a story about the picture.

Follow Me!

Please read to me.

God sent Jesus to you. Jesus told many stories about God's love. Many people came to hear Jesus tell stories. One day, a teacher asked Jesus, "What does God want me to do?" Jesus said, "Love God. And love everyone as much as you love yourself."

Based on *Mark 12:28–31*

Jesus said, "Come and see."
Jesus said, "Come, follow me.
Do as I do every day.
Show your love
in every way."

ACTIVITY

Draw yourself with Jesus.

SHOWING LOVE

I can follow Jesus.
I can show my love.

Color the hearts to show what you can do.

Make a bed

Set the table

Feed a pet

Say a prayer

FOLLOW JESUS

Let us sing.
Do what the children
*   in the pictures do as*
*   you sing.*

Follow Jesus.
Follow Jesus.

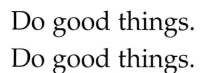

Do good things.
Do good things.

Love God and love others.
Love God and love others.

Show the way.
Show the way.

Let Us Pray

Thank you, Jesus, for
    showing us how to
    love God and others.
Amen.

Dear Family,

Your child began a new unit called "I Love God." Chapter 5 focuses on Jesus, who asks us to follow him by loving God and loving others.

At Home

Reinforce the faith belief that your child learned. A teacher once asked Jesus, "What does God want me to do?" Jesus replied, "Love God and love others the way you love yourself" (from *Mark 12:28–34*). Give your child opportunities to show love to others. Share your happiness when the child does.

Sharing Faith

Share the simple stories of Jesus with your child. Purchase a children's Bible; most bookstores carry a variety of choices. At bedtime, occasionally read from it a story about Jesus. Also, share your own favorite stories that tell ways that Jesus loved others. Affirm the times you see your child following Jesus. "You shared your toys. I'm so proud of you!"

Habits of Faith

Generosity. Develop an eagerness in your child to share. Give directives for sharing: "Here are two cookies. Pick one to share with your brother." "Here is a box of blocks. What can you and your friend build together?"

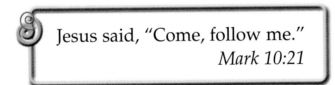

Jesus said, "Come, follow me."
Mark 10:21

Good Words

Let only
good words
come from
your mouths.

Ephesians 4:29

What Can They Say?

Look at the picture.
What good words can these
people say?

ICE CREAM 25¢

GROCERY

Good Words to Say

Here are good words to say every day.

Let me help you.

I'm sorry.

May I <u>please</u> have a snack?

<u>Thank</u> you.

I <u>love</u> you.

I CAN CHOOSE

I can use my mind to choose.

I can choose good words to say.

Look at the pictures.

Tell good words to say.

When you are angry

When you meet someone

When you cannot have your way

TALKING TO GOD

You can use good words when you talk to God.

Pick some good words.

Use these words to make up a prayer.

Please.   **I'm sorry.**

I will help.   Thank you.

Good Words to Pray

Color the spaces that have a star.
You will see the best words to pray to God each day.

Dear God,

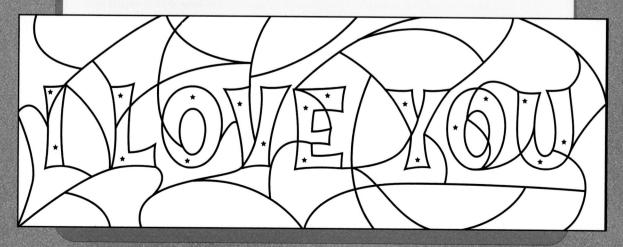

Dear Family,

Chapter 6, "Good Words," helped your child learn good words for showing love and providing care to others. These same words can be used when talking to God. Your child also learned that God gives people the ability to use their minds to make choices. Using good words is a good, respectful choice to make.

At Home

Take a few minutes to practice the use of good words with your child. For fun, use a doll, a stuffed animal, or an action figure. Act out what to say when you meet a new person, when you are angry, or when you want attention.

Sharing Faith

Make family prayer a part of your daily routine. Focus on mealtime blessings and bedtime prayers. Try to use both spontaneous prayers and traditional prayers. Check a religious bookstore or a Catholic web site for a book of family prayers. Try using the prayers on the back of these weekly letters as well.

Habits of Faith

Courtesy. Five-year-olds are very observant; it may seem as if their eyes are glued to you! Let your child hear you use courteous words and watch you do polite things. Show your child how to open a door for someone, how to shake hands when meeting a person, how and when to use words like "Please," "Thank you," "I'm sorry," or "Need some help?"

 Let only good words come from your mouths.
Ephesians 4:29

Good Things to Do

Grow in love for one another.

1 Thessalonians 3:12

Having Fun

Play is good!

God wants you to play with others.

Look at the picture.

Circle someone you would like to play with.

With a friend, act out how you would play.

The Lion's Friend

Can a great big lion and a little mouse become friends?
Listen to the story.

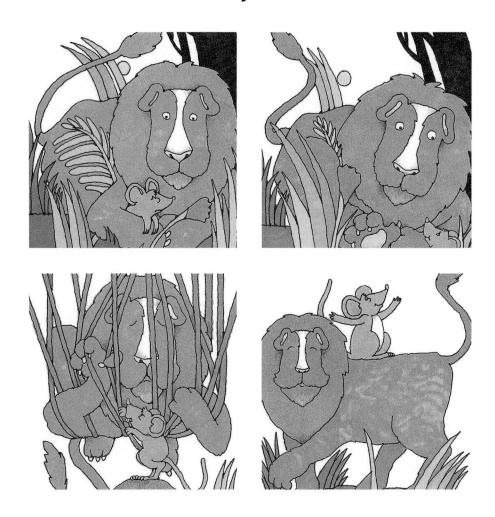

Wherever we go, whatever we do,
Never, ever will we part.
You're kind to me, and I'm kind
    to you.
That's how friendships start.

A Circle of Friends

Sit in a circle with your friends.
Swing your arms in and out as
   you say the poem.

Friends

Let's be friends.

Let's be friends in
   fair or stormy weather.

I will tell you something fun
   that we can do together.

PASS IT ON

Friends care for you.
Then you can care for others.
Show what you will do.

THE GOOD SHEPHERD

Please read to me.

Listen to the story Jesus told about being kind.

A shepherd had a hundred sheep. Every day, he took the sheep to eat sweet grass and to drink cool water. He kept them safe from wild animals.

One night, the shepherd counted his sheep. One sheep was lost! The shepherd left the other sheep in a safe place. Then he looked everywhere for the lost sheep.

The shepherd climbed rocks and crossed streams. He pushed through thorny bushes. The shepherd called and called.

At last, he found the sheep. He hugged the sheep and carried it back to the others. Along the way, the shepherd sang a song of thanks to God.

Based on *Matthew 18:12–14*

Thank you, Jesus. You care for me!

Dear Family,

In chapter 7, "Good Things to Do," your child explored the notions of friendship and kindness. Your child also learned that kind and caring actions are another way of showing love for God.

At Home

Caring for others is an important lesson at this age, and children take to it with gusto. But they do need help. Engage your child in cooperative play. Encourage your child to share toys and games with others. Read to your child or watch children's programs together. Many children's programs tell stories about friendship, sharing, and caring. You can provide the link between the stories and the faith. Remind your child how these kind actions show love for God.

Sharing Faith

Share with your child a time when you have been especially blessed by God. Remind your child that your own good actions show God your love. Tell about a saint who showed kindness, such as Saint Francis of Assisi. Retell the story of the Good Shepherd on the back of this page.

Habits of Faith

Kindness. Kindness can be shown in simple ways, such as sharing a smile with someone who's feeling blue or giving a hug when it's least expected. Affirm your child's acts of kindness: "You are so kind." Call attention to acts of kindness that you see in other people. Make kindness a word that's familiar to your child.

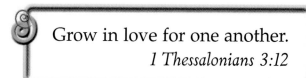

Grow in love for one another.
1 Thessalonians 3:12

I Can Pray

Pray always for all God's people.
Ephesians 6:18

Let's Talk!

Who do you like to talk to?
Who listens to you best?

Talking to God

What does it mean to pray?
Listen to Elena's prayers.

"Good morning, God.
I can't wait to play.
Be with me today."

"Thank you, God, for food
that helps us grow big
and strong."

"Dear God, I love you
this much."

"Dear God, this has been a great day.
Bless my family, especially my **abuela.**
I'm sorry that I teased Tomás and made
 him cry.
I'll try not to do that again."

"Dear God, help me take
good care of Bugsy."

"I really like Annie, God.
I'm glad she's my friend."

GOD LISTENS

God listens to you.

You can tell God anything.

Here is one way you can talk to God.

Sit as quiet as can be.

Close your eyes if you like.

Then talk to God in your thoughts.

Use the good words you know.

Tell God how you feel right now.

BLESS US, GOD

God blesses every person.
God keeps people in his care.
Say this blessing prayer together.

Bless us and help us, O God.

God, bless our families.

Help our families show love.

God, bless our friends.

Help our friends show kindness.

God, bless our neighbors.

Help our neighbors show care.

Think of someone you love.
O God, bless _____.
Keep him/her close to you.

Turn to the person next to you.
Place your hand on his or her head.
Say, **"God bless you, _____."**

Dear Family,

Chapter 8 focuses on prayer as a way of showing love for God. The children learned that prayer is a very natural way of talking to God and that a person can pray at any time, anywhere.

At Home

Prayer is part of who we are as Catholics. Be sure there are times for daily prayer in your home. Blessing prayers can remind you and your family that you are in God's special care. Perhaps before you eat a meal together or when you say good night, you and your child can spend a few moments asking God to bless special people in your lives.

Sharing Faith

The practice of blessing one's child is found in the Bible. Use this beautiful and intimate prayer in your family. You may wish to bless your child before he or she leaves for school in the morning. Or at bedtime, place your hand on your child's head, smile, and say, "God bless you and keep you safe."

Habits of Faith

Rituals. The Catholic Church is rich with celebrations of rituals and rites. Have one or two prayer rituals in your home. Make them suit your family's needs and your schedule. You may wish to invite a priest or a deacon from your parish to bless your home.

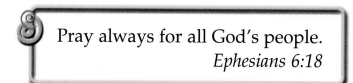

Pray always for all God's people.
Ephesians 6:18

I Love God

Jesus

Good Words

Good Things to Do

I Can Pray

All living creatures praise the Lord.

Psalm 150:6

Marshall Islands

From Maryknoll

I Love Others

Chapter

9 My Family

10 Friends

11 Being Together

12 Caring for Animals

My Family

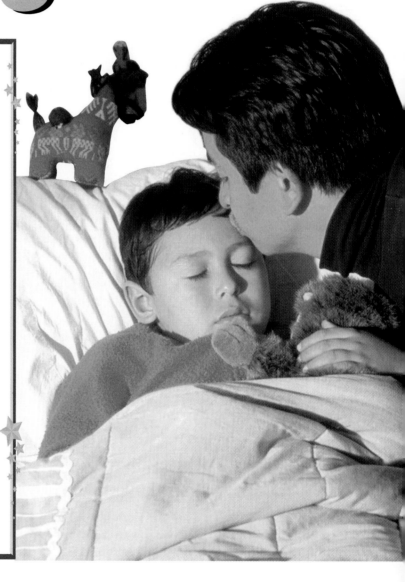

You Be *Good,* I'll Be *Night*

Please read to me.

You be the saucer,
   I'll be the cup,
   piggyback, piggyback,
   pick me up.
You be the tree,
   I'll be the pears,
   carry me, carry me
   up the stairs.
You be Good,
   I'll be Night,
   tuck me in, tuck me in
   nice and tight.
                  Eve Merriam

? **What do you like to do with your family?**

Many Kinds of Families

Families are the same in some ways.

The Yin Family
Father, Soo Lin, and Martin

The Arnold Family
Mama, Grandpa, Anne, and Holly

The Morales Family
Papa, Mama, Tina, and Luis

The Coleman Family
Mommy, Daddy, and Bill

Tell what these families like to do.
What does your family like to do?

Jesus and His Family

 *Please read to me.*

Jesus grew up in a family. Mary was his mother, and Joseph was his foster father. They all lived together in the small town of Nazareth. Joseph was a carpenter. He made things out of wood.

Jesus, Mary, and Joseph must have done all the things happy families do. They ate dinner together. They played and talked together. Each day, they set aside time to pray together. They thanked God for all their gifts. They asked God's help to do what was right.

Mary and Joseph loved Jesus very much. And Jesus loved them. They were a wonderful family. Jesus, Mary, and Joseph are called the Holy Family.

A Reflection on *Luke 2:39–40*

What are some things Jesus liked to do with his family?

WITH MY FAMILY

Draw something you like to do with your family.

HOORAY FOR FAMILIES

Hip, hip, hooray for families!

Families talk and play together.

Hip, hip, hooray!

Families cook and clean.

Hip, hip, hooray!

Families take care of one another.

Hip, hip, hooray!

Families visit their
    relatives.

Hip, hip, hooray!

Families welcome
    their friends.

Hip, hip, hooray!

Thank you, God,
    for giving me
    a family.

Amen.

Dear Family,

Chapter 9 focuses on the concept of family. Your child learned that family can be defined in many ways. He or she was introduced to the model of the Holy Family, and perhaps can tell you something about Jesus, Mary, and Joseph.

At Home

Celebrate being a family. Time pressures seem greater today, but the basic needs of children do not change. Set aside quiet time with your child each day, especially at bedtime. Listening carefully to your child and letting your child know that you value him or her is the greatest gift you can give—and it doesn't cost money!

Sharing Faith

Your parish church may have a statue of the Holy Family, or at least separate images of Mary and Joseph. Visit your church and point out these reminders of the Holy Family. Be sure your child is familiar with the names Jesus, Mary, and Joseph. Talk together about Jesus growing up in a family and the ways it would be similar to life in your family.

Habits of Faith

Family Time. In addition to time spent with your immediate family, your child also needs to feel a part of any extended family you may have. If close relatives live far away, help your child to know these family members through photos, cards and letters, and occasional phone calls. At large family gatherings, remember that your child may not feel at ease with relatives he or she does not know well. Give your child special tasks. He or she can help set the table for a meal or share family pictures or a special drawing.

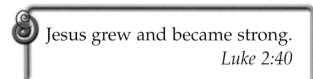

Jesus grew and became strong.
Luke 2:40

FRIENDS

MY FRIEND AND ME

> **Treat others the way you want them to treat you.**
>
> *Matthew 7:12*

We go together
   like butter on
   and hair on a head.

Like macaroni and
   and dimples on knees.

Like berries in a
   and (you pick one)
   stars in the sky,
   a shirt and a tie,
   ham on rye.

We're as close as can be,
   my friend and me!

JESUS IS MY FRIEND

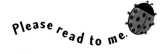

Please read to me.

Jesus had been teaching all day long.
   ("Hooray!")
Jesus sat to rest.
   ("Hooray!")
Children wanted to get close to Jesus.
   ("Hooray!")
Some grown-ups said, "Stay away!
Jesus is too tired!"
   ("Oh, no!")
But Jesus said, "Let the children come
to me."
   ("Hooray!")
Then he hugged the children.
   ("Hooray!")
The children were happy to be with
their friend Jesus.

From *Mark 10:13–16*

Be a Friend

There are many ways to be a
   friend.
Do you share toys?
Do you take turns?
Do you help pick up when the
   game is over?

Jesus told how to be a good friend.
Jesus said, "Treat others the way
   you want to be treated."
How about that!

FRIENDS SHARE

Draw lines to show ways to share.

MY PRAYER

Thank you, God, for my friend
_____.
Help me be a good friend.
I will share.
I will be kind.
I will help my friend.
Amen.

MY PROMISE

I WILL BE YOUR GOOD FRIEND.

Dear Family,

Your child is gradually leaving a me-centered world and moving out toward others. Chapter 10, "Friends," acknowledges this transitional stage. Your child discovered that Jesus is a friend, and discussed ways to be a friend to others.

At Home

A good sign of friends playing together is the sound of laughter. Laughter, a way of releasing tension and expressing joy, is essential to healthy living. Your child, however, will need some guidance to see the difference between laughing *with* someone and laughing *at* someone.

Sharing Faith

Your child learned about friendship from Jesus who taught the Golden Rule, "Do to others whatever you would have them do to you" (*Matthew 7:12*). There are many times during the day when you can help your child live this way. Ask your child, "How would you feel if this happened to you?" or "How do you think he (she) feels?" Questions like these help your child understand the other person's point of view.

Habits of Faith

Fairness. This virtue is at the heart of the Golden Rule. Fairness can be difficult to accept, particularly for young children, who are very literal. Try to limit the meaning of fairness to obvious situations, such as following the rules when playing a game or including others in play.

 Treat others the way you want them to treat you.
Matthew 7:12

Being Together

The followers of Jesus gathered together. They all helped one another.

Acts 2:44–45

The Clubhouse

Please read to me.

Nicky and Sarah sat in their favorite spot.

They sat under a tall oak tree.

The tree's long, droopy branches shaded them from the sun.

"I like it here," said Sarah. "Let's turn this tree into a clubhouse!"

Nicky said, "OK. My dad has some scraps of wood we can use."

"Let's ask Jacob and Mark, too," said Sarah.

Jacob brought cardboard boxes.

Mark dragged over a wooden chair.

Before long, Rachel came by with a blanket.

The friends were on their way to making a great secret hideaway.

Wouldn't a clubhouse be fun? Draw yourself in the picture.

A Neighborhood

Most people live in families. Families live in neighborhoods. People try to make their neighborhood a good place to live.

Choose something in the picture. Tell a story about it.

A New Family

The Miller family is moving into the neighborhood.

A long moving van is parked outside their new home.

Can you imagine all that's inside?

The van is stuffed with boxes.

Furniture is squeezed into spaces.

There is a lot of work to do!

What would you do to help?

WHAT I CAN DO

I live in a community.
I can show love and care in a way
that is just right for me.

How are these children being
good neighbors?
How can you be a good neighbor?
Draw what you will do.

A STORY

Dear Jesus,
Help me be a good neighbor.
Amen.

"I don't want to help."

"Someone else will help."

"I will help."

Dear Family,

Chapter 11 continues the unit theme of loving others. In this chapter, your child explored the concept of the neighborhood. Understanding the neighborhood as community lays the foundation for your child's understanding of the Catholic Church as a community of believers.

At Home

Involve your child in ways to contribute to the community—throwing away trash instead of littering, obeying city rules, respecting community helpers. To familiarize your child with your community, point out the local fire department or police station. Help him or her to appreciate the work of rubbish collectors, road maintenance workers, and the local fast-food workers. Take the family to a special event in your parish. Look at a community paper and point out photos of familiar places.

Sharing Faith

Your child discovered that the people in a neighborhood need to help one another. Play "Let's Pretend" and ask your child to make up the "best neighborhood." It may be easier for your child to draw a picture and then use it to explain his or her ideas. Whenever your child talks about elements of sharing, caring, or helping in the community, point out that this is how God wants people to live.

Habits of Faith

Good Neighbors. In some neighborhoods, it's easy to be a good neighbor. In other neighborhoods, it may be more difficult to find a way. Whatever your living situation, model good manners and a pleasant attitude toward your neighbors.

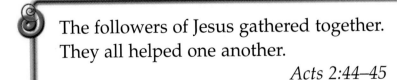

The followers of Jesus gathered together. They all helped one another.

Acts 2:44–45

Caring for Animals

God gave people
the care of all
the animals.

Genesis 1:26

The Animal Dance

Prance like a horse,
   clip, clop.
Slink like a tiger,
   swish, swish.
Stomp like an elephant,
   boom, boom.
Flutter like a finch,
   flap, flap.
Pounce like a puppy,
   boing, boing.
Hop like a bunny,
   hippity, hoppity.
That's how you do
   the Animal Dance!

God's Creatures

God has filled the world
with wonderful animals.
Will you be the caretaker?
Help some animals find a
a home that's just right.

Do you have a pet?
Would you like to have one?
What would you choose?

Draw your pet or one you would
   like to have.
Show how you would care for it.

WE GIVE THANKS

 lives in a  and sings pretty .

 does tricks and makes us all day long.

 gives us , so cool and so .

 gives us wool for our 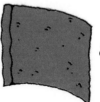 at .

Thank you, God, for all the animals.

I will help care for them.

Amen.

Dear Family,

Children learn much about life from their relationships with animals. Caring for animals teaches them valuable lessons that they will carry over into their relationships with others.

At Home

Caring for a pet is often a child's first significant responsibility. If you have an animal in your home, let your child share in its care. Don't expect more than a five-year-old is capable of doing. If you don't have a pet, take opportunities to help your child discover the wonder of animals. Go to a park or a zoo. Watch birds flutter, squirrels scamper, ducks bob for food—all make our world a marvelous place.

Sharing Faith

In the Bible, the story of Creation tells of God giving people dominion over the earth. (See *Genesis 1*.) And so, the care for living things is a religious as well as a social responsibility. Help your child treat animals with respect and experience the good feelings that will result.

Habits of Faith

Gentleness. Gentleness is the opposite of violence. Some young children treat animals in ways that may cause the animals pain or harm. Be sure to make it clear that this behavior is never acceptable. Model gentleness with animals you know to be safe. Teach your child to avoid animals that may pose a danger.

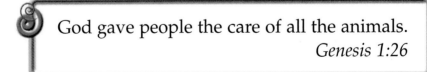

God gave people the care of all the animals.
Genesis 1:26

I LOVE OTHERS

My Family

Friends

Being Together

Caring for Animals

Jesus said,
"Come,
follow me."

Mark 10:21

Zambia

 From Maryknoll

Church

Chapter

13 I Belong

14 My Parish

15 My Father's House

16 I Am Catholic

I Belong

Good for Me!

I belong to my family.

You are the Church.

1 Corinthians 3:16

I belong to my
_____
school.

I belong to my
_____
church.

I Go to Church

I belong to a church.
We gather every week for Mass.

We have fun together.

We do things for others.

We pray together.

WELCOME TO MY CHURCH

God calls everyone.
You are welcome at my church.

Draw yourself here.

ALL ARE WELCOME

Form a line to sing this song.
Clap and march while you sing.

All are welcome at our church,
   at our church,
   at our church.
All are welcome at our church.
We're so happy!

You're Welcome

Decorate the welcome sign.

Dear Family,

Your child began the unit titled "Church." In chapter 13, your child was introduced to the concept of belonging to the Church.

At Home

Do a little exploring with your child. Find things in your home that identify you as a particular family. Perhaps your family name is on the mailbox or on a decorative sign. Photos and photo albums also identify your family and show who belongs. Tell your child, "We are the *(your last name)*."

Sharing Faith

Now do a little exploring for objects that show you and your family belong to the Church, such as a cross, a palm branch, or the Bible. When you point out an object to your child, use sentences that reinforce your child's Christian identity. For example, you can say, "This Bible shows that we belong to the Church."

Habits of Faith

Hospitality. Hospitality is a virtue that the followers of Jesus have practiced since the early Church. Give your child opportunities to perform simple acts of hospitality—welcoming visitors, asking them to sit down, helping to serve them refreshments. Remind your child that welcoming others is an important part of belonging to the Church and following the way of Jesus.

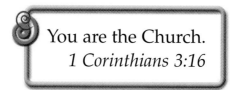

You are the Church.
1 Corinthians 3:16

My Parish

> **I will praise you, Lord, with all my heart.**
>
> *Psalm 9:2*

Cookie Time

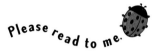

Please read to me.

Tony said, "I like making cookies with you, Nana." Tony plopped teaspoons of dough onto a shiny cookie sheet.

Ring! There went the timer! Nana smiled at Tony. She put on thick cotton mitts and pulled a tray out of the oven. The chocolate chips were popping through the cookies like warts on a frog.

"Mmm, mmm, good!" said Tony, as he tasted one. "Nana, let's invite Mr. Garcia over to have some, too."

Write a friend's name on the cookie.

My Parish Family

I belong to a parish.
Draw a line from the house to the parish church.
At the end, you will see another name for the Church.

My parish is part of the People
  of God.
We meet in a church.
We pray to God there.

GOD LOVES ME

Please help me play.

Here is a girl named Jessica.

(Hold up index finger.)

Here is a boy named Carlos.

(Hold up other index finger.)

Carlos and Jessica meet some other children.

(Hold up all fingers.)

All the children walk into church.

(Walk all ten fingers.)

The children sit side by side.

(Fold hands, interlock fingers.)

Carlos and Jessica stand up to sing.

(Raise index fingers.)

The other children stand up to sing.

(Press all fingers together.)

Now look at your hands.

This is one way to pray!

My parish is called _____.

A LITANY PRAYER

GROUP 1: We are God's People.

GROUP 2: Let's be kind to others.

GROUP 1: We are God's People.

GROUP 2: Let's stop and give help.

GROUP 1: We are God's People.

GROUP 2: Let's love God and others.

GROUP 1: We are God's People.

GROUP 2: Let's pray for families and friends.

GROUP 1: We are God's People.

ALL: Let's give thanks to the Lord.

Dear Family,

Chapter 14, "My Parish," focuses on the Christian community the children know best—the parish. They don't understand the difference between Church with a capital *C* (the People of God) and church with a lowercase *c* (the building).

At Home

Talk about some of the things you like to do as a family—the meals you share and the fun times you have. Establish family rituals—perhaps you always have pancakes after Sunday Mass or you drive to a field to pick out Halloween pumpkins.

Faith Sharing

Talk about the ways God's People show they are a community of love. Help your child name some of the ways. They go to Mass. They show kindness to others. They pray. They give help. Then, together, decide on a specific way you will show kindness or give help during the week.

Habits of Faith

Prayer. Try to form a habit of family prayer. Even the custom of a mealtime blessing is a start. When a family member is ill or is facing a difficult time at work or school, try gathering for a minute or two and asking the Holy Spirit to make him or her strong. The power of the Holy Spirit was given to the Church, and you are the Church of the home.

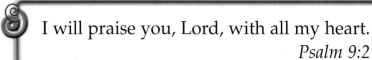

I will praise you, Lord, with all my heart.
Psalm 9:2

My Father's House

INVITATION **15**

Come in, let us
bow down and
praise God.

Psalm 95:6

A Special Place

See the door.

Where can it be?

Turn the page.

And you will see.

My Father's house is

a good place to be.

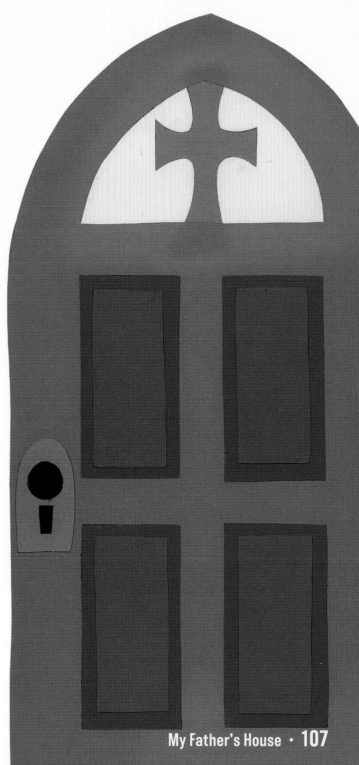

Inside the Church

My Father's house is a church.
See the holy things.
Holy things help you pray.

Pews

Holy
Water

Baptismal
Font

WHAT BELONGS?

Circle the things that belong in church.

A HAPPY PLACE TO BE

Listen to bells ring
  "ding-a-ling, ding-a-ling."
They are like voices that sing
  "Come to church, come to church."

Music begins with a
  booming sound.
People stand and sing out.
What a happy place to be!

We Pray

The priest says, "The Lord be with you."
We say, "And also with you."

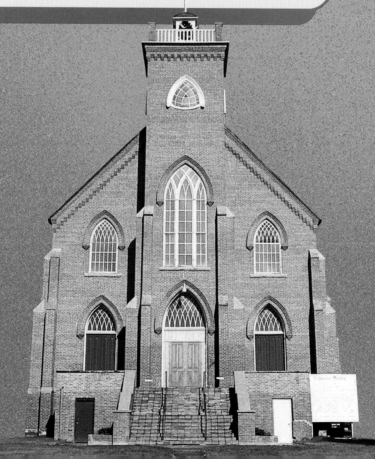

Dear Family,

"My Father's House" is the title of chapter 15. The chapter introduced your child to some of the "holy things," or sacramentals, that are used in Catholic prayer and worship. The sacramentals in a church, such as the cross, the altar, and the statues, are reminders of God.

At Home

Help your child choose an age-appropriate holy object, such as a statue or picture of a guardian angel, to put in his or her room. Or sit with your child while he or she draws something of a religious nature to display. If your child already has a religious item, share some information about it, such as who gave the item and when it was received. Display a cross as a symbol of faith.

Faith Sharing

When you are at Sunday Mass, be sure your child sees the host and the cup. Spend a few minutes after Mass to notice other holy things—the altar, the crucifix, the statues, the holy water, and the stations of the cross. Name each object, too. Then, briefly talk about the ways in which these holy things remind you of God's presence and help you pray.

Habits of Faith

Reverence. Holy things are handled with special care, with reverence. Model reverence for your child. Show your child how to handle the Bible and how to make the sign of the cross with holy water. Point out the ways in which the priest and the others performing special ministries at Mass show reverence for holy objects.

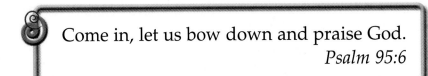

Come in, let us bow down and praise God.
Psalm 95:6

I Am Catholic

Family Words

Circle words that mean family.

mommy   brother   papa   firefighter

daddy   grandmother   teacher   sister

dinosaur   grandfather   uncle   zookeeper

Catholic

Catholic is a church word, too.
You are a Catholic.
You belong to the Catholic
   Church.

SING ALLELUIA!

In church, the priest reads
a story about Jesus.
Before he reads, everyone
sings.
They sing, "Alleluia!"

Hold your hands high.

Praise the Lord from the ☁ .
Praise the Lord, ☀ and 🌙 .
Praise him, all you shining ⭐ .

Hold your hands low.

Praise the Lord from the 🌸 .
Praise the Lord, you ⛰ and hills.
Praise the Lord, you animals and 🐦 .

Stretch your arms wide.

Praise the Lord, all you 👥 .
All the rich and the poor,
All the young and the old,
Praise the Lord!

From *Psalm 148*

Dear Family,

Chapter 16 is titled "I Am Catholic." Kindergarten children find their identity in the words they use. Words give them a sense of belonging, too. Children enjoy the experience of learning the common language of the groups they belong to. Show your child how proud and happy you are to belong to the Catholic Church, to worship together at Mass, and to use the language of faith.

At Home

Help your child recognize the importance of knowing and using the words and phrases that identify your family as a Catholic family. Don't limit yourself to just words from the Mass. Talk, too, about the priests, the sisters, the deacons, and others in the parish. Refer often to the saints, the Blessed Mother, and the like. Your Catholic conversation will help your child grow in a sense of Catholic identity.

Sharing Faith

The best way to help your child recognize and feel comfortable with words of faith is to use them. Begin your mealtime blessings with the sign of the cross. Teach your child to close bedtime prayers with "Amen." Point out the "Alleluia" as it is sung at Mass and invite your child to sing along.

Habits of Faith

Keep God's Name Holy. Five-year-olds love to mimic the words they hear, especially if they have an idea that the words may cause a reaction. Model proper use of God's name. Be sure that your child understands that God is holy, and so God's name is holy. God's name should not be used in anger or meanness.

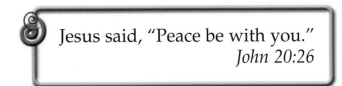

Jesus said, "Peace be with you."
John 20:26

Unit 5

God, I am
always in
your care.

Psalm 31:15

South Korea

From Maryknoll

Celebrate

Chapter

17 **Memory**

18 **Being Alive**

19 **Holy Days**

20 **The Mass**

120

Memory

Family Stories

Families remember stories.
Can you remember a family story?
Tell your family story.

Use Your Memory

Put on your thinking cap!
What can you find in your memory?

Remember a time you were scared.

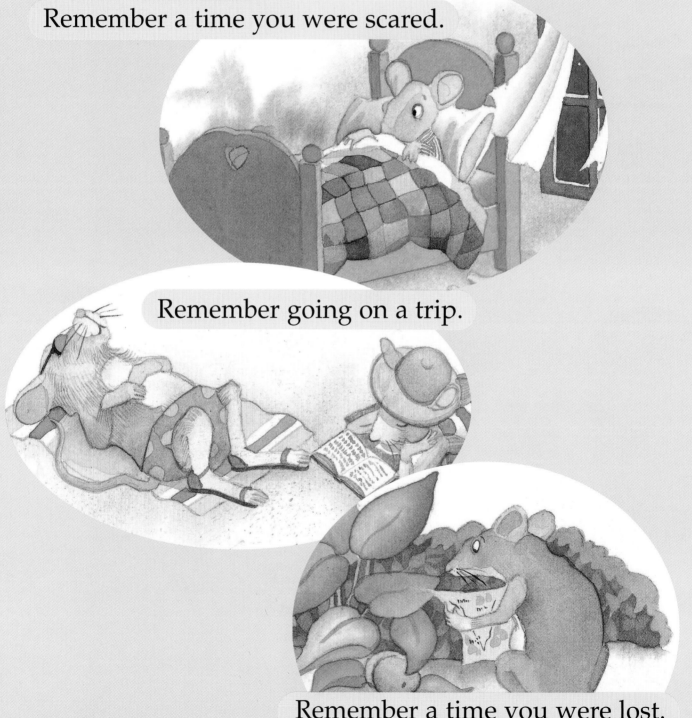

Remember going on a trip.

Remember a time you were lost.

Remember your last birthday.

Draw your best memory ever!

STORIES OF JESUS

Look at the pictures.
Tell what you remember.

Zacchaeus

The Good Shepherd

The Holy Family

Draw a Jesus story you remember.

REMEMBERING JESUS

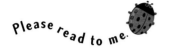

Please read to me.

Jesus was in a house with his friends. He was telling them stories and teaching them lessons. The house was very crowded.

Outside there was a very sick man. His friends wanted Jesus to make the man better. But they could not get through the door of the house. What could they do?

They climbed on the roof. They cut a hole in the roof. They lowered the man down—bed and all—into the house.

Jesus smiled. "Pick up your bed," he said. "You can go home now." Jesus made the man well.

From *Luke 5:17–25*

Thanks for Memory

Thank you, Jesus, for giving me my
   memory.
Help me remember you always.
Amen.

Dear Family,

The new unit, "Celebrate," lays groundwork for an understanding of the Mass. Because the Mass is a remembrance of Jesus, the subject of chapter 17 is memory. Families share and celebrate memories. The Church shares memories by proclaiming the Scriptures at Mass and by repeating the words and the actions of the Eucharist.

At Home

On slips of paper, write words that trigger family memories—*vacation, birthday, Christmas,* and the like. Fold the slips and ask each family member to pick a slip and to share a memory triggered by the word.

Sharing Faith

Share a short Scripture story with your child. If you are more comfortable reading a story, use a children's Bible. Libraries and bookstores have several to choose from. Choose simple stories that have nothing frightening or confusing to a child. Children love the stories of Zacchaeus (Luke 19:2–10) and the Good Shepherd (Luke 15:4–7 and John 10:12–18). They will enjoy hearing them again and again.

Habits of Faith

Biblical Faith. The teachings and the traditions of the Catholic faith have their source in Scripture. Catholics today are encouraged to read and to pray the Bible, for it is there that all will find the story of God's presence and the simple message of Jesus that brings life. Try to read the Bible every day. Tell your child why you do.

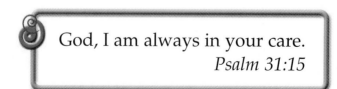

God, I am always in your care.
Psalm 31:15

Being ALIVE

> **I give you thanks that I am alive.**
>
> *Psalm 139:14*

Tell about You

How old are you?

_____

- - - - - - - - - -

    I am _____ years old.

Tell what you can do.

Tell what you can learn.

What songs can you sing?

What games can you play?

    _____

- - - - - - - - - -

    I like being _____ years old!

A Day to Celebrate

Many people were happy the
day you were born.
Friends and family welcomed you.
Your birthday is a day to celebrate.

Sing

Play

Draw and color in the balloons.
Show how you celebrate your
    birthday.
Talk about what you do.

Invite

Eat

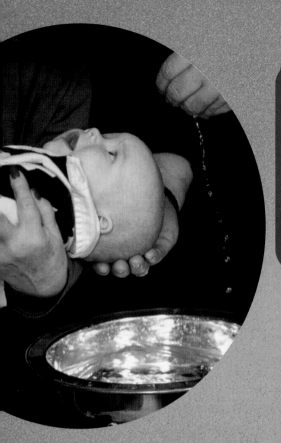

WELCOME

The Church welcomed you into
God's Family.
You were welcomed at Baptism.
Your baptism was a happy day.

BAPTISM

A QUIET PRAYER

Listen and pray.
Sit quietly.
Think about your birthday.
Think about Baptism, too.
Color the candles.

Thank you, God, for my life.
Thank you, God, for my
   baptism.
Thank you, God, for
   welcoming me.

Dear Family,

Christian celebration is based on hope in new life. Chapter 18 begins by focusing on the celebration of a birthday—a celebration children love. Then the chapter turns to the celebration of Baptism.

At Home

Tell how happy you were the day your child joined your family. When a family birthday celebration is near, let your child help plan it. If you wish, start a birthday ritual. Use your child's age to write a list: "Five Things I Love Best about You." Add to the list each year.

Sharing Faith

Baptism marks each person's birthday into the Catholic community. Share pictures or mementos of your child's baptism. Tell why you chose the godparents you did. Help your child keep in touch with them. If you still have the baptismal candle, light it on the anniversary date of the baptism.

Habits of Faith

Respect for Life. Birthdays celebrate God's gift of life. Help your child see that all people are children of God and that each person's life should be respected. If you have the opportunity, point out that disabilities—blindness, deafness, paralysis, and mental problems—are part of human life.

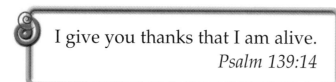

I give you thanks that I am alive.
Psalm 139:14

Holy Days

**Praise the Lord,
who is so good.**

Psalm 136:1

A Noisy Day

It is the Fourth of July.
Americans have a party.
They have parades.
They listen to music.
They eat good food.
They watch fireworks.
The Fourth of July is a holiday.
It is a very noisy day.

Celebrations

Look at the quilt.
Circle three patches.
What are the people celebrating?

Christmas

PEDRO

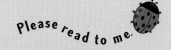

Please read to me.

There are different ways to celebrate the Christmas feast. Listen to two of those ways.

1. Rosa and Pedro live in Mexico. (Find the pictures of Rosa and Pedro.) They decorate their home with green plants and paper lanterns called luminarias. (Find the luminarias.) On Christmas Eve, Rosa puts a statue of the baby Jesus in the manger. (Find the baby Jesus.) Rosa and Pedro take turns breaking the Christmas piñatas. (Find the piñatas.) On Christmas Day, Rosa and Pedro go to church with their whole family. (Find their church.)

ROSA

2. Flor and Nacasio live in the Philippines. (Find Flor and Nacasio.) During Christmastime, they put on plays about the birth of Jesus. (Find the Christmas scene.) Flor and Nicasio make Christmas lanterns and carry them in the Christmas parade. (Find the lanterns.)

FLOR

NACASIO

Holy Days • **135**

CHURCH DAYS

The Church celebrates days of remembering.

These days are called holy days.

On holy days, the Church remembers Jesus or Mary or one of the saints.

Easter and Christmas are holy days.

EASTER

Draw an Easter picture.

CHRISTMAS

Draw a Christmas picture.

WE GIVE THANKS

After each line, do a little dance and wave your streamers.

Give thanks to the Lord, who is so good.
Celebrate and give thanks to the Lord!

We give thanks for holy days.

We give thanks for the gift of Jesus.

We give thanks for everyone here.

We give thanks for _____.

Give thanks to the Lord, who is so good.
Celebrate and give thanks to the Lord!

Dear Family,

Chapter 19 talks about holidays and holy days, days for remembering and for celebrating. Holidays are enjoyable times, and your child will soon see that the Church's holy days can be fun, too.

At Home

Every family has its own traditions. Ethnic traditions are passed on from one generation to another. They help identify who you are. Share with your child how your traditions came about. If your family is short on special celebrations, start a new one. Every tradition began somewhere.

Sharing Faith

Christmas and Easter are holy days. Keep their religious meaning alive in your family. Let your child know that Christmas and Easter are days of remembering Jesus—when he was born and when God raised him from the dead.

Habits of Faith

Celebrations. The Church sees all of its gatherings as celebrations. To your child, celebration may mean a party with presents. You can broaden your child's understanding by creating some simple ways to celebrate being a family. You can have a cup of hot chocolate along with a bedtime story. Or make the ornaments for your Christmas tree.

 Praise the Lord, who is so good.
Psalm 136:1

The Mass

Remembering Gramps

Please read to me.

> **Wherever you are gathered in my name, I am with you.**
>
> *Matthew 18:20*

Every year, the Franco family gets together on the day Gramps died. They laugh about the jokes Gramps told. They talk about the birdhouses Gramps made. Someone brings spaghetti and meatballs. Gramps said there was nothing better to eat! The Franco family likes to remember Gramps.

? **How does your family remember members who have died?**

Sunday Mass

Every Sunday is a holy day.
The parish family gets
    together every Sunday.
The parish celebrates Mass.
The parish remembers Jesus.

1. Coming to Mass

2. Greeting the people

3. Singing together

4. Listening to God's Word

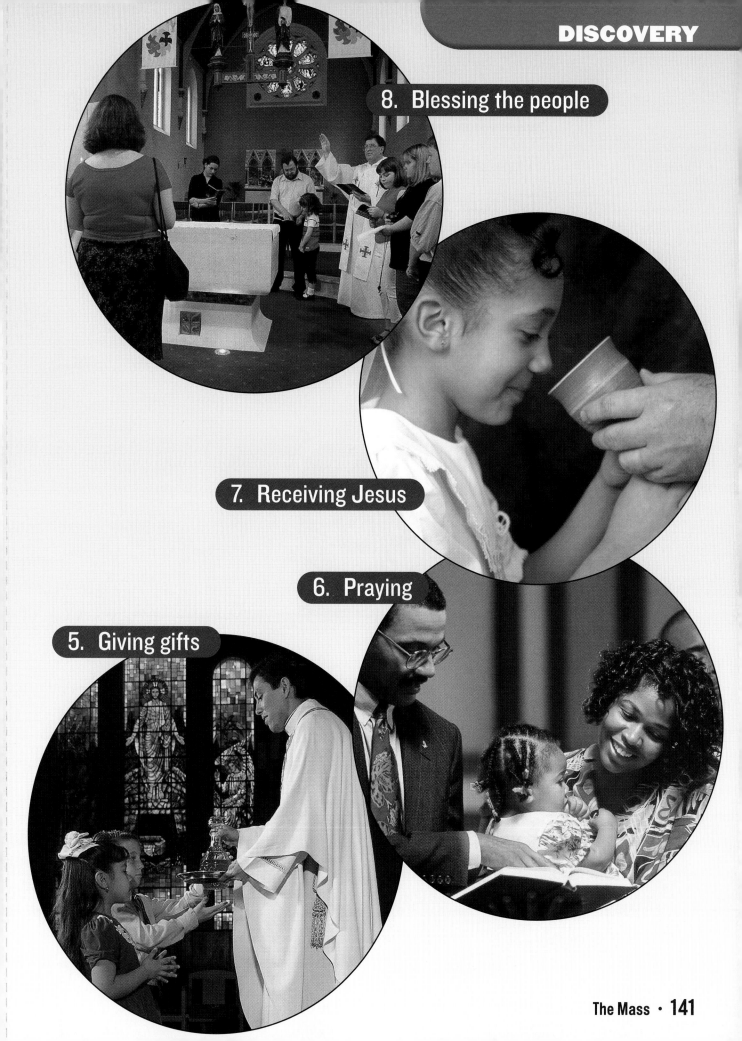

8. Blessing the people

7. Receiving Jesus

6. Praying

5. Giving gifts

SERVING AT MASS

The priest leads the people at Mass.
Ushers greet the people.
The choir and the musicians make music.
The servers help the priest.
Everyone has something to do.
Draw what you do at Mass.

WALK AND PRAY

Oompah! Oompah! Oompah-pah!
Parades are fun!
Horns toot.
People march and wave.

There are church parades, too.
People walk in a long line.
They sing and praise God.
A church parade is called a
   procession.

Have a procession.
Pray while you walk.
Sing "Alleluia," too.

Alleluia

Dear Family,

In chapter 20, your child was introduced to the Mass as an important way to remember Jesus.

At Home

Involve your child in helping the family get ready for Sunday Mass. Perhaps your child can choose the Mass to attend and get his or her clothing ready the night before. On Sunday, leave for Mass in an unhurried way so that tension is not associated with going to church.

Sharing Faith

Sunday is a holy day that recalls Jesus' life, death, and resurrection. Every Sunday gather with God's Family to celebrate the Mass. Do what you can to involve your child. Introduce your child to the priest. Speak the responses clearly and with conviction. Every Mass response is an expression of faith. Sing together. Smile a lot and show that you enjoy going to Mass.

Habits of Faith

Discipline. Sometimes it's easy for Mass attendance to fall off when you have small children at home. If you have an outside job as well, Sunday may be your only day to stay home. However, the Sunday Eucharist is the heart of Catholic life. Try to make the obligation of Sunday Mass attendance a family event. Eat together or go on an outing after Mass. Such traditions become happy memories and enrich faith.

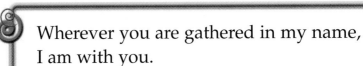

Wherever you are gathered in my name, I am with you.

Matthew 18:20

CELEBRATE

Memory

Being Alive

Holy Days

The Mass

Grow in love for one another and for all.

1 Thessalonians 3:12

San Andres Sajcabaja

 From Maryknoll

Caring

Chapter

21 Be a Helper!

22 Care

23 Caring for You

24 The Good of All

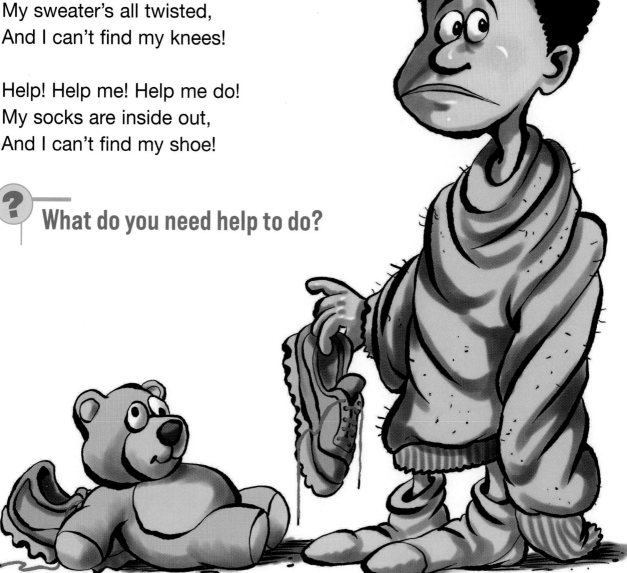

> Jesus said,
> "Help others,
> and you
> help me."
>
> *Matthew 25:40*

Be a Helper!

I Need Help!

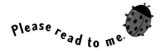

Please read to me.

Help! Help me! Help me, please!
My sweater's all twisted,
And I can't find my knees!

Help! Help me! Help me do!
My socks are inside out,
And I can't find my shoe!

? **What do you need help to do?**

Helping Hands

Sometimes you need help.
Sometimes you can help others.

Play the game.
It will remind you to
   help others.

THE
HELPING
GAME

Start

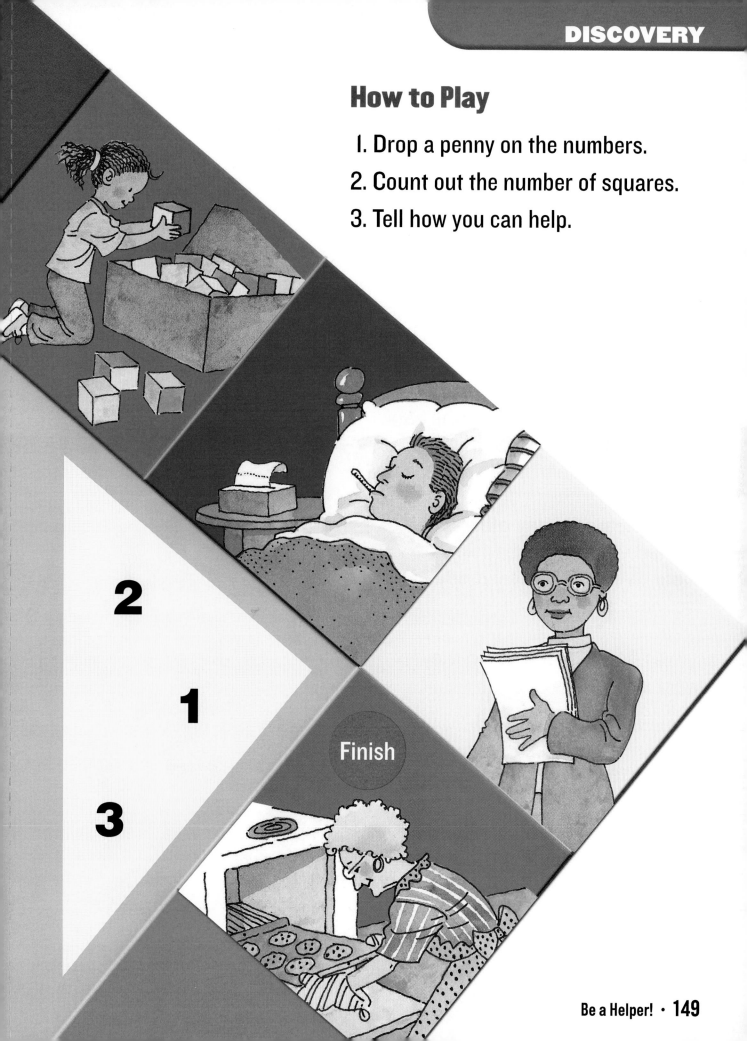

How to Play

1. Drop a penny on the numbers.
2. Count out the number of squares.
3. Tell how you can help.

2

1

Finish

3

JESUS CHOSE HELPERS

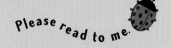
Please read to me.

Jesus wanted to tell people about God's love. Jesus needed help. "Come with me," Jesus told two brothers, Peter and Andrew.

They said, "Yes, Jesus!" And they went with Jesus.

Jesus needed more helpers. "Come with me," Jesus said to James and John. "I want you to help me."

James and John said, "Yes, Jesus!" And they went with Jesus.

Jesus called many others. "I need you all," Jesus told them. "We will tell everybody we meet about God's great love."

"Yes," they all said. And they went with Jesus.

From *Matthew 4:18–22*

Jesus needs your help, too!

A HELPING PRAYER

I will help.

I use my to help you look.

I use my to set the table.

I use my to run an errand.

I will for people, too.

Jesus, I promise to help!

A helper of Jesus! Hooray! Hooray!

Dear Family,

Chapter 21 is titled "Be a Helper." Your child learned that Jesus invites others to help him in his work of telling people about God's great love. Caring for others is a way of showing love for God.

At Home

Trace your child's hand on a sheet of paper. Decide on one or two jobs that your child can do to help the family. Print the jobs in the hand. Acknowledge when each job is done, and say how thankful you are to have such a good helper. Affirming when a job is done will be more effective than complaining when it isn't.

Sharing Faith

Get involved in your parish in whatever way your time allows. This sets a good example for your child. Be sure not to use church work as an excuse for not being with your child. That sets up resentment. If your parish invites families to bring up the gifts at Mass, be sure to volunteer.

Habits of Faith

Helping. Your habit of helping others is the best lesson your child can get. Involve your child with helping others whenever you can. Perhaps you and your child can collect the neighbor's mail when he is away. Perhaps you can donate clothing to a mission. Your child can help you with washing and folding clothing. You get the idea.

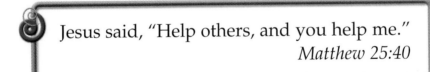

Jesus said, "Help others, and you help me."
Matthew 25:40

CARE

Love and care for one another.

John 15:12

Being Kind

Kitty said, "No one is kind to me!"
Willa Gorilla said, "Kitty, I will be
kind to you!"

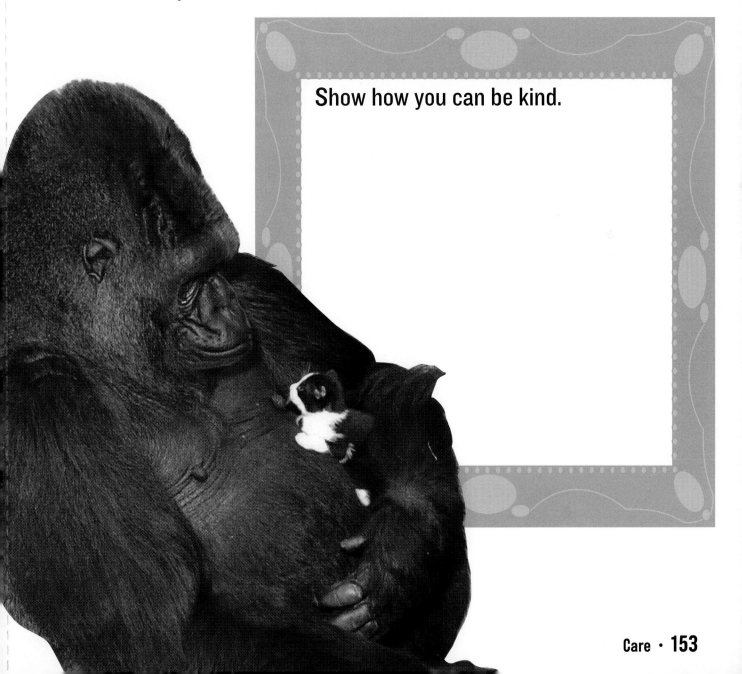

Show how you can be kind.

JESUS CARED

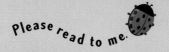

Please read to me.

Jesus cared about children. He cared about mothers and fathers. He cared about teachers and tax collectors, too.

Jesus understood people's feelings. He knew what made people sad. He knew what made people happy.

Jesus said, "I love and care for all of you. Love and care for one another."

From *John 15:12*

You can learn about the care Jesus has for you. Jesus will help you love and care for others.

SHOW YOU CARE

Look at each picture.
Tell how the children
show they care.

I will show that I care.

KIND AND CARING

ALL: Let us pray. We ask for God's blessings for those who need care. We ask him to make us kind and caring.

READER: For those who are hungry and for those who are cold.

CHILDREN: Bless them, Lord! And make us kind and caring.

READER: For those who are lonely and for those who are sad.

CHILDREN: Bless them, Lord! And make us kind and caring.

READER: For those who are sick and for those who are dying.

CHILDREN: Bless them, Lord! And make us kind and caring.

ALL: Amen.

Dear Family,

Chapter 22, "Care," helped your child to identify concrete ways of showing care and kindness for others. The lesson also told more about Jesus and how he truly cared for the feelings and the misfortunes of those around him. All are asked to live as Jesus lived.

At Home

Make a list of all the people who are kind to you and your family—no kindness is too trivial. Talk about the list in general. Then ask your child to point to one name and to tell how that person shows kindness and care. Share with your child a specific way you have seen his or her caring and kindness.

Sharing Faith

Remind your child that Jesus cared for all people. Ask your child to name ways that he or she can care for others. The conversation may bring up examples of children in kindergarten who are not kind and caring. Without judging the other children, point out that you want your child to be kind and to show care.

Habits of Faith

Care. Go back to the kindness list you and your child made. Guide your child to think of a simple way to return kindness to one person on the list. You don't have to come up with complicated schemes—simple is better.

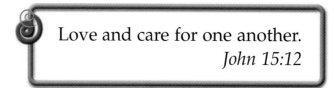

Love and care for one another.
John 15:12

Caring for You

Growing Up

Babies can't do much.
Somebody has to feed
   them.
Somebody has to wash
   them.
Somebody has to rock
   them.

You are growing up.
You are learning to
   take care of yourself.

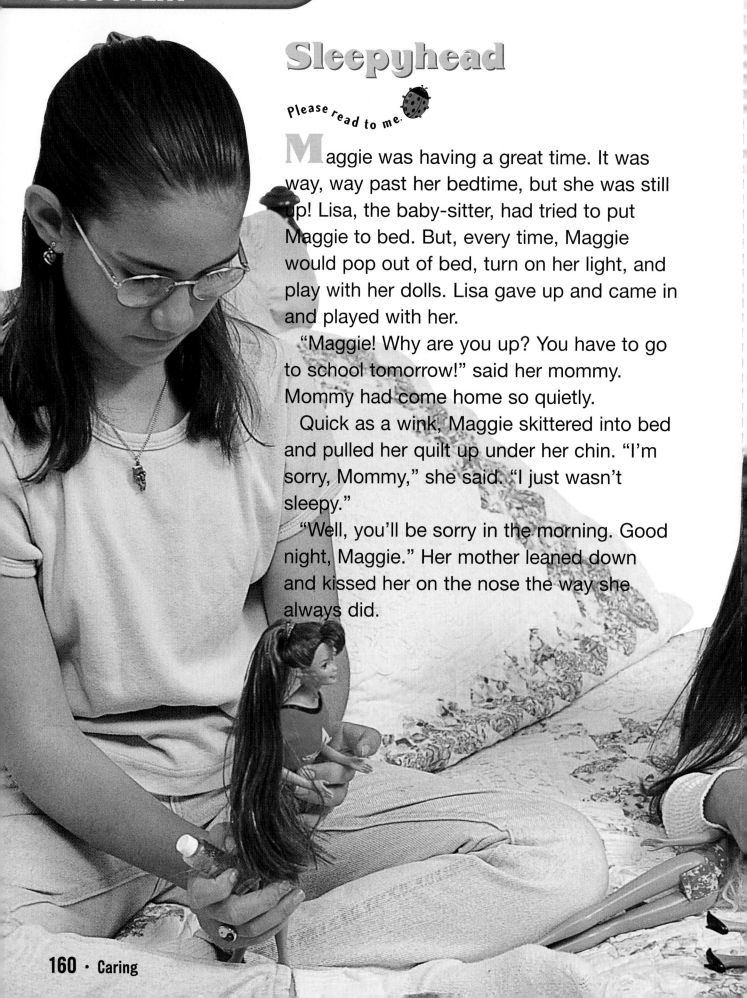

Sleepyhead

Please read to me.

Maggie was having a great time. It was way, way past her bedtime, but she was still up! Lisa, the baby-sitter, had tried to put Maggie to bed. But, every time, Maggie would pop out of bed, turn on her light, and play with her dolls. Lisa gave up and came in and played with her.

"Maggie! Why are you up? You have to go to school tomorrow!" said her mommy. Mommy had come home so quietly.

Quick as a wink, Maggie skittered into bed and pulled her quilt up under her chin. "I'm sorry, Mommy," she said. "I just wasn't sleepy."

"Well, you'll be sorry in the morning. Good night, Maggie." Her mother leaned down and kissed her on the nose the way she always did.

The next morning, Maggie felt fine. She didn't feel sorry at all. She skipped all the way to school.

In the story circle, the teacher was reading a new book about a rabbit and a bumblebee that became friends. "Friends with a bee?" Maggie thought. Then she yawned. She was very, very sleepy.

Maggie woke up with a start. "And the rabbit and the bumblebee sighed with relief," said the teacher, closing the book. "That had been a close call!"

Maggie looked around. What had happened in the story? Maggie had slept through the very best part!

You need lots of sleep.
You need good food and exercise, too.
Part of growing up is learning to take good care of you.
How do you take care of you?

CARE FOR GOD'S GIFT

Your body is a gift from God.
God wants you to care for his gift.
You can keep clean.
You can get lots of sleep.
Don't forget to eat good food, too.

Taking care of your body is a way to say
   "Thank you, God!"

Follow the Right Path

Use a crayon.
Follow the best path.
See how to care about you.

SAFETY RULES

God wants you to be safe.
You can follow the safety rules.

Say no to strangers.

Ask someone you trust for help.

Find a friend to walk with you.

Every day, ask God to keep you safe.

Keep Us Safe

Dear God,
Keep us all healthy.
Keep us all safe.
Make us happy and full of love.
Amen.

Dear Family,

Your child has grown and changed since infancy. Ideally, as human beings grow, their physical growth is coupled with an ability to understand and be attentive to their own needs and the needs of others. Chapter 23, "Caring for You," taught your child that it is important to care for themselves with good personal habits.

At Home

A concrete way your child can show self-respect is through the exercise of good health and safety habits. You have a most important role in the development of such habits. Remind your child how necessary it is to take care of the gift that God has given. Make a personal checklist for your child. On the checklist write the daily "musts" of rest, good food, dental hygiene, exercise, and so forth. Make sure that you use positive reinforcement when the child follows the checklist.

Sharing Faith

Be careful how you reprimand your child. Remember to find fault with the action, not with the person. For example, it is better to say "Hitting your sister is not a good thing to do" than it is to say "You are so bad because you hit your sister." Assure your child that your love, like God's, is constant and is never withdrawn.

Habits of Faith

Gratitude. Make the expression of thankfulness a common occurrence. End each day with your child with a simple thank-you prayer. As you thank God for the blessings of the day and for the special people in your lives, include a prayer of thanks for the gift of your child.

 Try always to do what is good and pleasing to God.
Romans 12:2

The Good of All

We can share our gifts for the good of all.

1 Corinthians 12:7

Not Alone

You are not alone.

God created a great big world.

God's creatures need you.

Look at the plant.

Color the leaves that show what the plant needs.

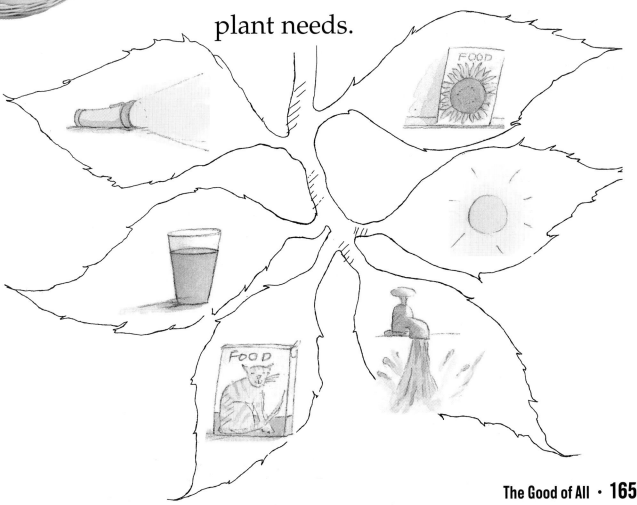

Needing People

I need you, and you need me.
And that's the way it's supposed
   to be.

Circle any two people on the
   page.
Make up a story.
Tell how the people need each
   other.

Who Needs You?

Look at the stars.
Pick two stars.
Tell what you see.
The pictures tell that people need
   you!
Decorate the stars.

Family

Friends

Pet

Teacher

DOING GOOD

Look at us!
We are doing good!
When we do good,
everyone is happy!

Good Together

1. Trace your hand on a sheet of paper.
2. Get two other children to trace a hand on your paper.
3. Name the picture "We Do Good Together!"

A GOODNESS PRAYER

Repeat each line the leader says.

1. Hello, my friends!
2. Let's all join hands.
3. Let's do good together.
4. We'll think of others.
5. We'll do what's best.
6. Let's do good in the summer.
7. And we'll do good in fall.
8. We'll do good for others.
9. We'll love and care and grow!
10. Amen, amen, amen!

Dear Family,

Your child ends the kindergarten religion classes with the chapter, "The Good of All." A simple ditty summarizes the chapter. You may find it useful in parenting: "I need you, and you need me. And that's the way it's supposed to be." Kindergarten children are still learning that their actions affect others. This chapter plants the seeds of working for the common good.

At Home

Say the prayer on the other side of this page. This method of praying is a good way for parents to pray with their children. You can do this repetition—usually referred to as a call and response—with many familiar prayers. Don't be afraid to say the prayer almost like a cheer.

Sharing Faith

Talk about how good it feels inside to be needed and how good it feels to do something for someone in need. Doing things for others often doesn't cost money. Time and attention can be the best gifts of all. Point out to your child that often what a person needs is a smile.

Habits of Faith

Peace. Today's world often assaults the senses. One of the great treasures today is quiet time. Analyze the pattern of evening activity in your home. Try to establish a quiet time shortly before bedtime. Children are as much in need of winding down as adults are. Wind down together. Eventually this may turn into prayer time. At the very least, it will lead to a better night's sleep!

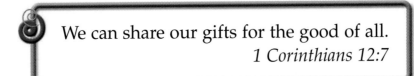

We can share our gifts for the good of all.
1 Corinthians 12:7

CARING

Be a Helper!

Care

HELP THE HOMELESS

Caring For You

The Good of All

Celebrate!

Praise the Lord, all people.

Psalm 47:1

Mother Mary
·
All Saints
·
Advent
·
Christmas
·
Lent
·
Easter
·
Summer

Mary is the mother of Jesus.
Mary is your mother, too.

Mother Mary

You can learn Mary's prayer.

I will praise the Lord with all my
  heart.
(Stretch your arms up high.)
I will tell of God's great works.
(Stretch your arms wide.)

I will be glad and thank you, God.
(Cross your arms over your heart.)
I will praise your name, Lord God.
(Bow your head.)

**Color the
picture of
Mary.**

Saints are special friends of
Jesus.
Saints have a special day.
It is All Saints' Day.
Color the picture of the saints.
Let's celebrate.

Me, Too!

I am a friend of Jesus.
I love Jesus very much!
I am happy to belong to God's
Family.

ook at the Advent wreath.
Color a leaf every day.
Soon it will be Christmas.

There are four weeks in Advent.
Each week you will color a candle.
Each week you will say a prayer.

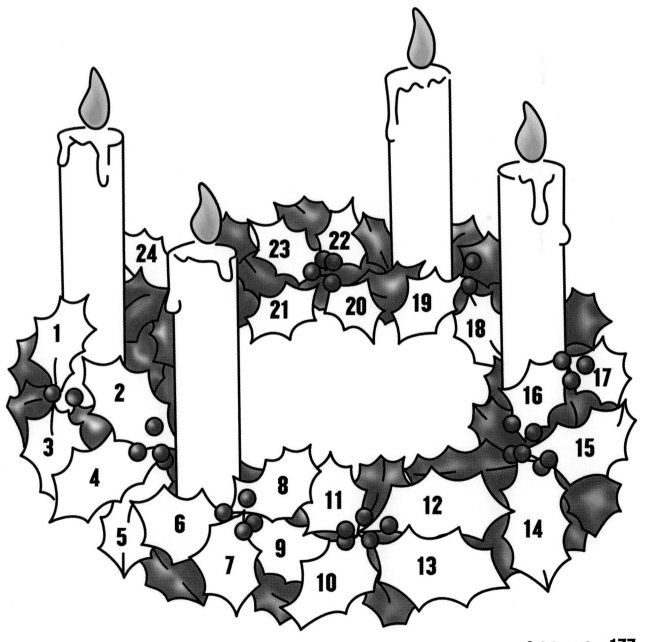

An Advent Prayer

Dear Jesus,
We are waiting, waiting, waiting.
We are waiting to celebrate the
  day you were born.
We get ourselves ready.

Week One
Add:
We try to be kind.
Jesus, help us use kind
  words.
Amen.

Week Two
Add:
We try to share.
Jesus, help us share.
Amen.

Week Three
Add:
We try to help.
Jesus, let us help at
  home and at school.
Amen.

Week Four
Add:
We try to care.
Jesus, help us be
  kind to others.
Amen.

Christmas is Jesus' birthday.
Happy birthday, Jesus!

Merry Christmas!
Decorate the tree.
Sing a Christmas carol.

Silent night! Holy night!
All is calm, all is bright
'Round yon virgin Mother and Child.
Holy Infant, so tender and mild,
Sleep in heavenly peace,
Sleep in heavenly peace.

See the birds.
See the flowers.
Soon, it will be spring!

Listen

Lent is a time to pray.
God listens to your prayers.
You can talk to God about
   anything.
You can listen to God, too.

Draw a prayer for Lent.

Easter is a happy day.
Easter is a day for new life.
Match the signs of new life.

Easter is a day to say "Alleluia!"

Easter Egg Hunt

Color the picture.

See how many Easter eggs you
   can find!

Summer is a time to play.
Look at the pictures.

I dance and sing.

I jump and run.

I play with others.

Summer is a time to pray, too.
Look at the pictures.

I talk and sing.

I stand and kneel.

**Praise the Lord
with shouts of joy!**

I pray with others.

**Now make a reminder.
It is good to play and to pray.**

A is for Advent.
We wait for Jesus.
And **A** is for altar, the table in church.

B is for Baptism.
And **B** is for Bible, the book of God's Word.

C is for Christ—a name for Jesus.
And **C** is for caring, for Christmas, church, and cross.

E is for Easter—the day Jesus rose.
And **E** is for Eucharist—a name for the Mass.

187

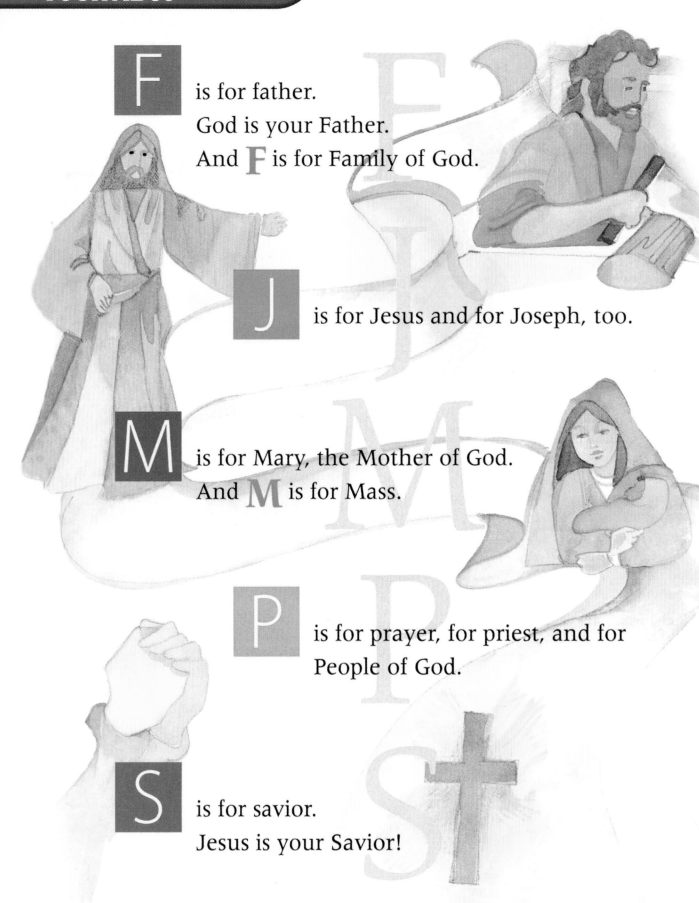

F is for father.
God is your Father.
And **F** is for Family of God.

J is for Jesus and for Joseph, too.

M is for Mary, the Mother of God.
And **M** is for Mass.

P is for prayer, for priest, and for People of God.

S is for savior.
Jesus is your Savior!

There are many more letters and words to know!

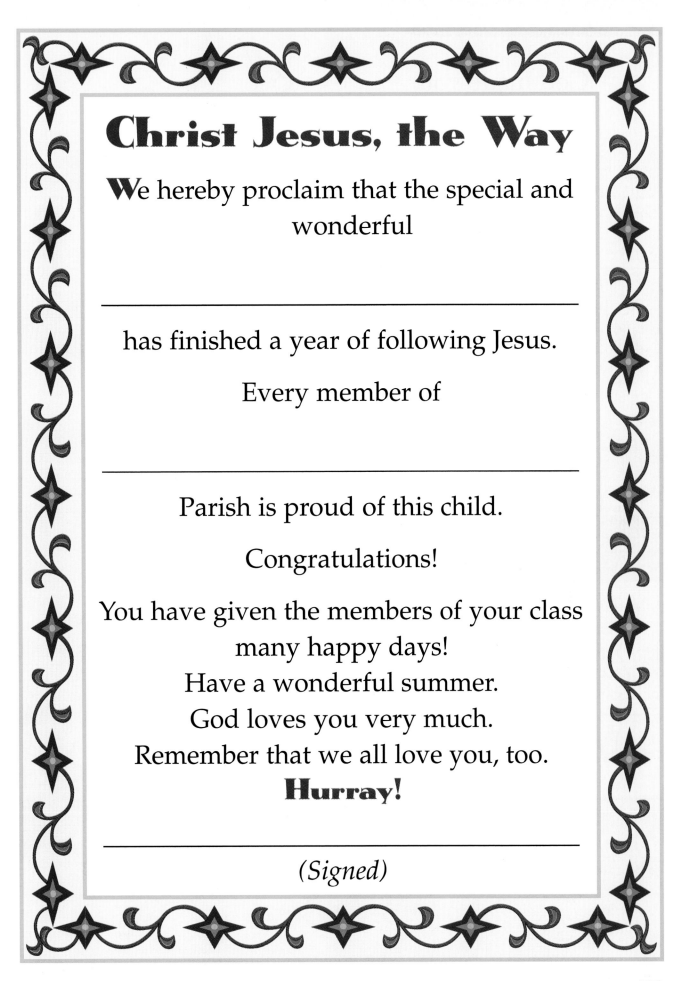

Christ Jesus, the Way

We hereby proclaim that the special and wonderful

_____

has finished a year of following Jesus.

Every member of

_____

Parish is proud of this child.

Congratulations!

You have given the members of your class many happy days!
Have a wonderful summer.
God loves you very much.
Remember that we all love you, too.
Hurray!

_____

(Signed)

God made you.
I do believe!

The world is God's gift to you.
I do believe!

God is your Father.
I do believe!

Jesus is God's Son.
I do believe!

You belong to God's Family.
I do believe!

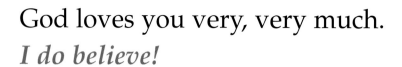

God loves you very, very much.
I do believe!

God wants you to be happy forever.
I do believe!

Hurray, God!

ACKNOWLEDGMENTS

Illustrations Winky Adam: 107; Linda Clearwater: 175; Eldon Doty: 147, 166, 169; Jim Effler: 36–37, 57; Kate Flannigan: 23, 29, 50, 51, 55; Amanda Harvey: 20, 24, 25, 27, 35, 165; Dennis Hockerman: 110; Pat Hoggan: 65, 81; John Jones: 41, 67, 93, 119, 145, 171; Anthony Lewis: 4, 6, 18–19, 78; Terra Muzick: 117, 128–129, 131, 133; Christi Payne: 21, 53: Julie Peterson: 135; Doug Roy: 39, 47, 62, 63, 82–83, 102–103, 134; Susan Spellman: 13; Peggy Tagel: 75; Bonnie Matthews: 88–89; George Ulrich: 5, 95, 96–97, 98, 99, 101, 104, 108–109, 130, 142, 148–149, 162

Photographs Cleo Photography: 64, 130, 131, 140–141; Payl Barton/Stock Market: 121; Maryknoll Brothers/Maryknoll Photo: 16; C. Squared Studios/PhotoDisc: 165; Alan and Sandy Carey/PhotoDisc: 87; Dr. Ronald H. Cohn/Gorilla Foundation/Koko. Org./Gorilla Foundation: 153; Corbis: 111; Stewart Cohen/Tony Stone Images: 52; Peter Correz/Tony Stone Images: 32; Deborah Davis/PhotoEdit: 32; Donna Day/PhotoDisc: 52; DigitalVision: 27; Laura Dwight/Photo Edit: 156; Kathy Ferguson/Photo Edit: 156; Myrleen Ferguson Cate/PhotoEdit: 32, 61, 140–141;

Sr. Janet Hockerman/Maryknoll Photo: 68; Jack Hollingsworth/Photodisc: 137; Richard Hutchings/PhotoEdit: 32; Don & Liysa King/ImageBank: 84; Sr. Bernice Kita MM/Maryknoll Photo: 146; Rob Lewine/Stock Market: 113; Tony May/Tony Stone Images: 52; Br. John M.N./Maryknoll Photo: 120; MaryKnoll Photo: 42; Ryan McVay/Photodisc: 127; Michael Newman/PhotoEdit: 69; Kevin Peterson/Photodisc: 32; Photodisc: 17; PhotoLink/PhotoDisc: 77, 133, 156; Andreas Pollock/Photo Edit: 157; Tom Raymond/Tony Stone Images: 140–141; Helene Rogers/Art Directors and TRIP Photo Library: 140–141; Rubberball Productions/Stockmarket: 90; Don Smetzer/Tony Stone Images: 84; Ariel Skelley/Stock Market: 139; Stock Market: 32, 75; SW Productions/PhotoDisc: 43; Jacob Taposchaner/FPG International: 5, 84; Kevin Thomas/Maryknoll Photo: 94; Ross Whitaker/ImageBank: 32; David Young-Wolff/Photo Edit: 160–161; David Young-Wolff/Tony Stone Images: 105; Eric Wheater/Maryknoll Photo: 94

191

Name Tag

Take-home Badge

Special Glasses

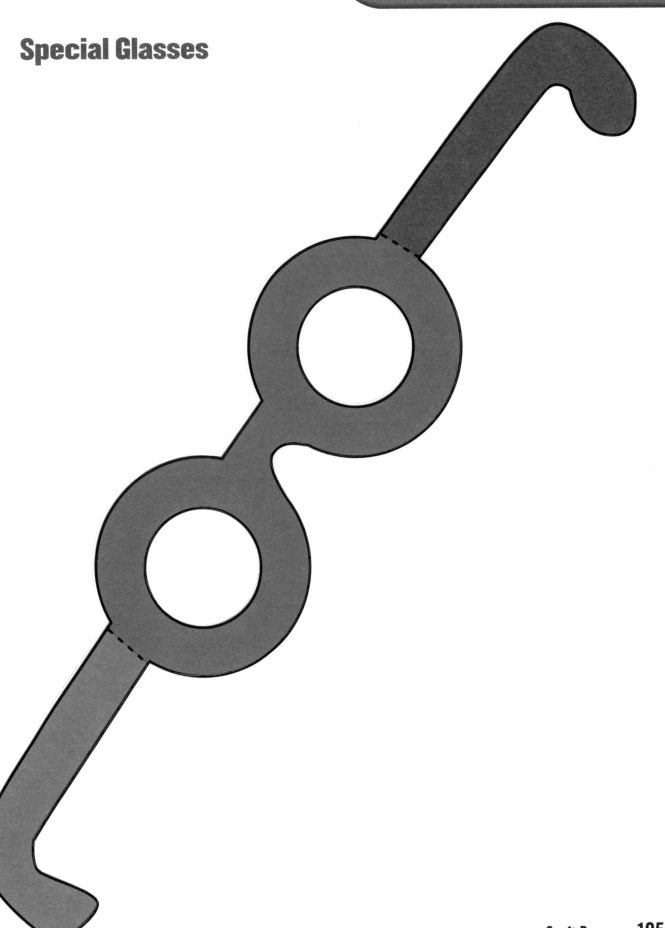

Prickly Porcupine

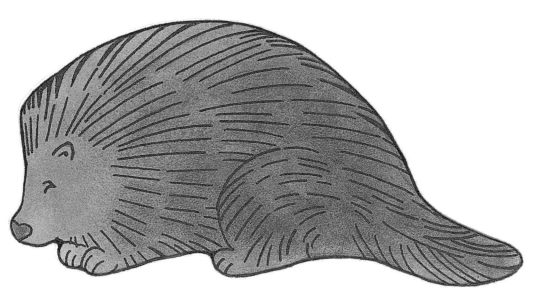

Flying Bird

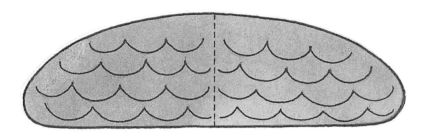

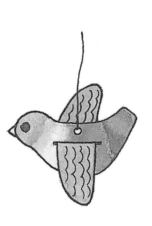

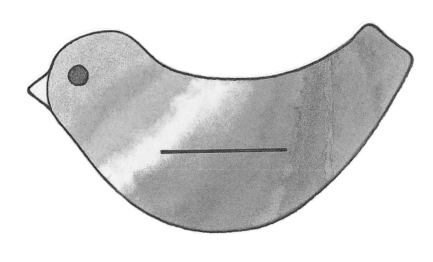

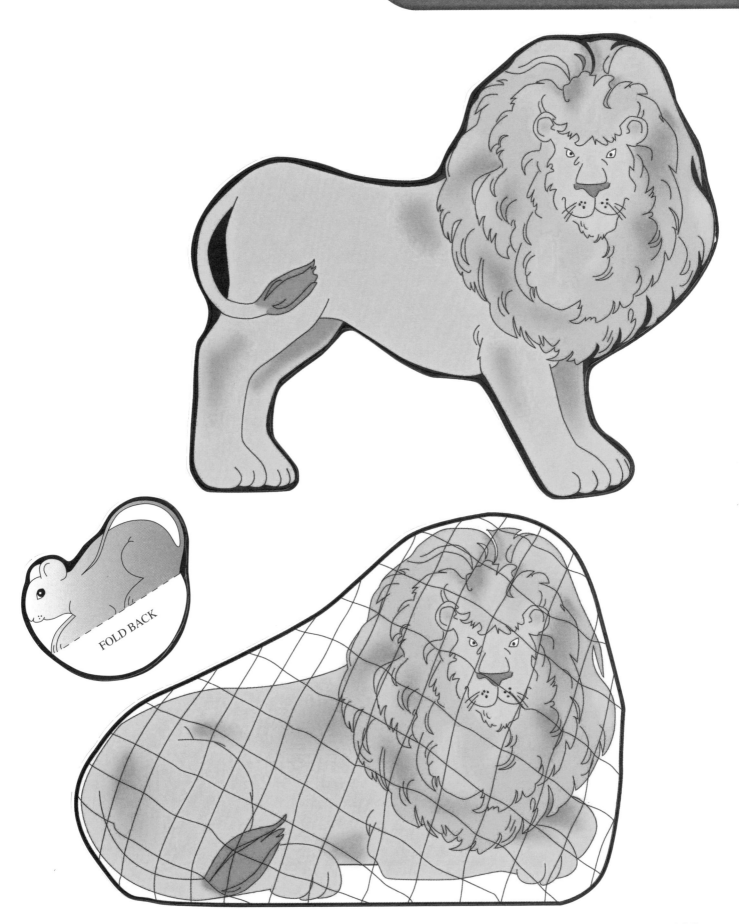

FOLD BACK

Lord, hear my prayer!

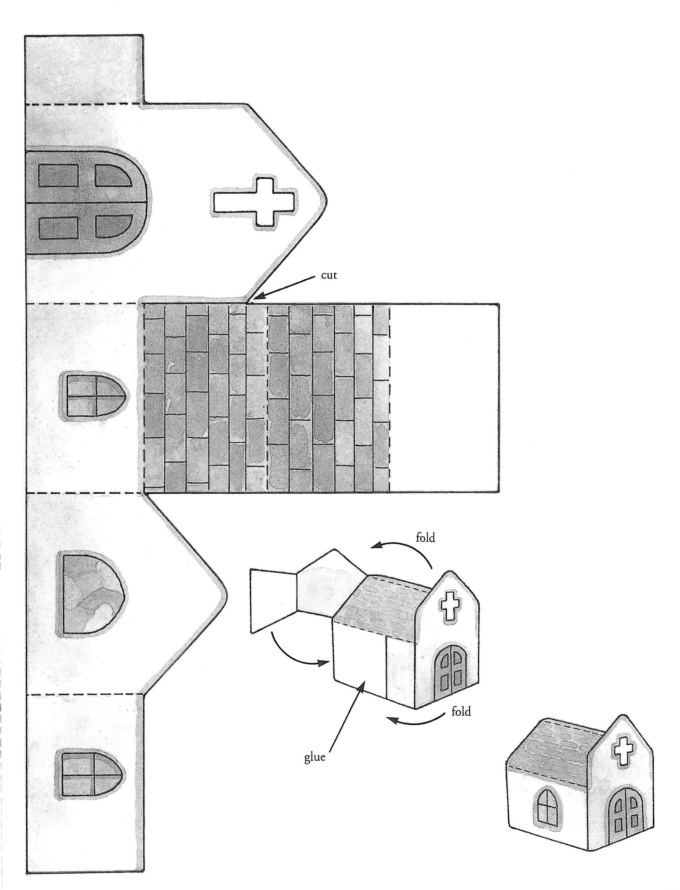

cut

fold

fold

glue

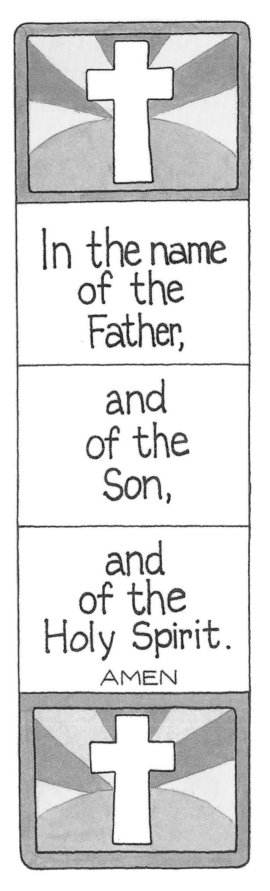

In the name
of the
Father,

and
of the
Son,

and
of the
Holy Spirit.
AMEN

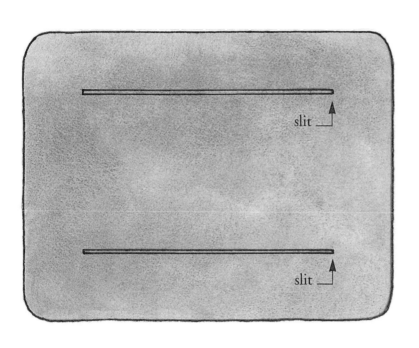

slit

slit

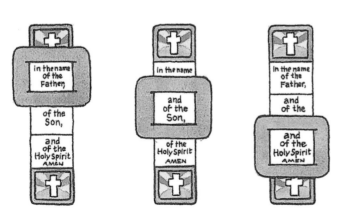

slit

slit

Fold end sections
inside

My
Helping
Hand

Caterpillar

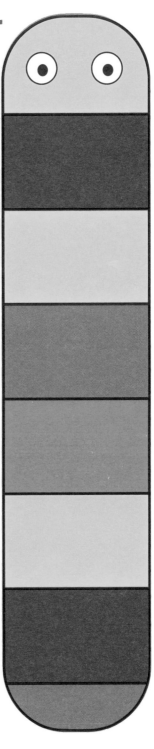

Cocoon

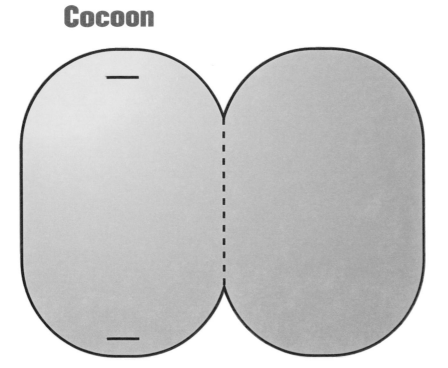

Butterfly

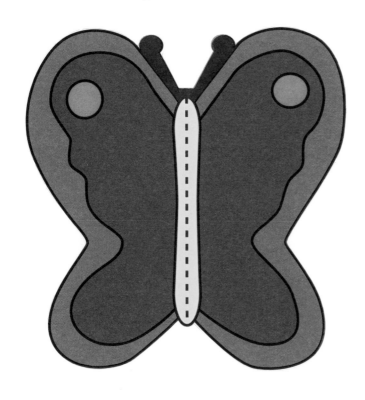